THIS BOOK BELONGS TO